T0419206

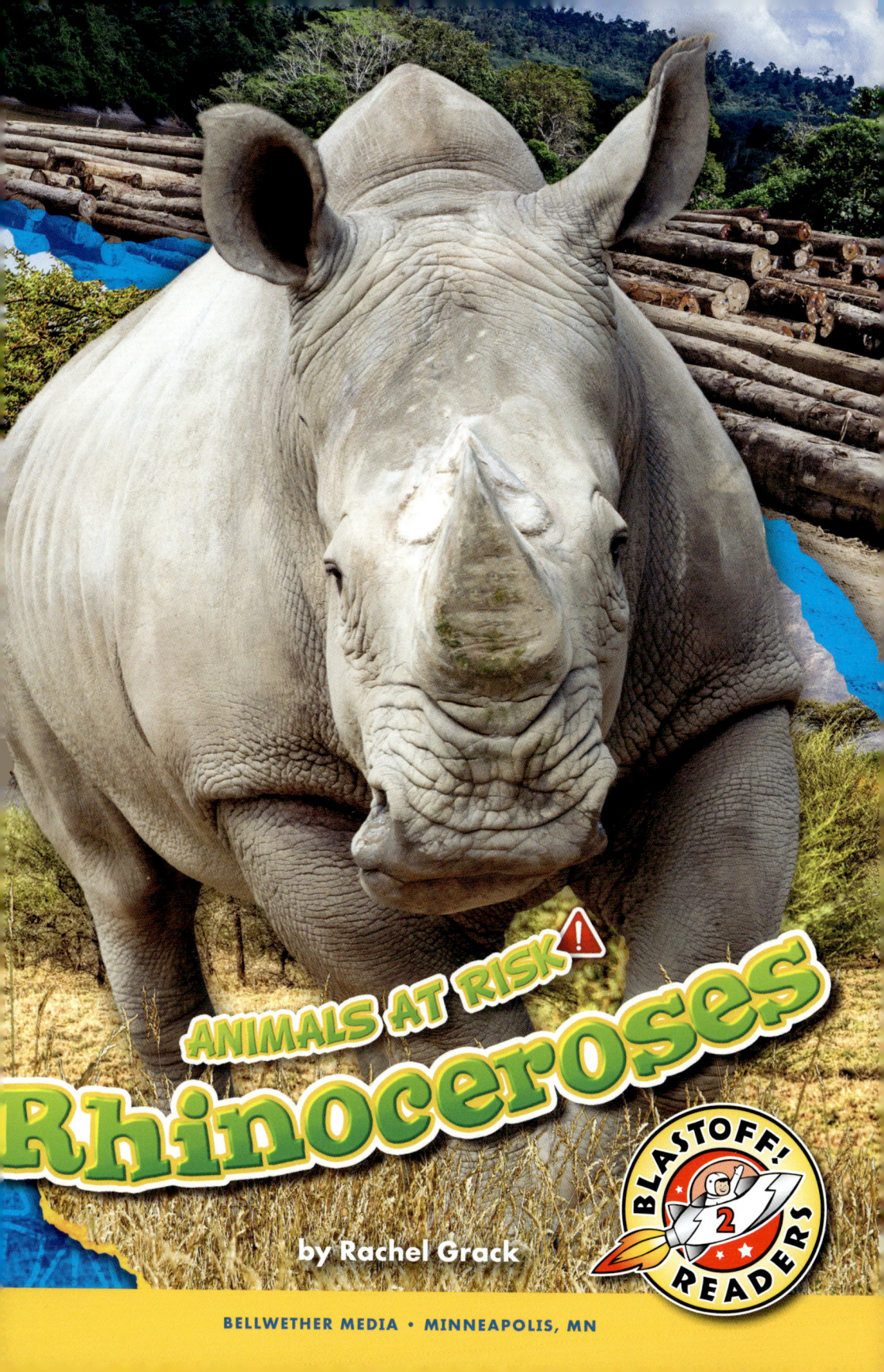

ANIMALS AT RISK ⚠️

Rhinoceroses

by Rachel Grack

BLASTOFF! READERS 2

BELLWETHER MEDIA • MINNEAPOLIS, MN

Blastoff! Readers are carefully developed by literacy experts to build reading stamina and move students toward fluency by combining standards-based content with developmentally appropriate text.

Level 1 provides the most support through repetition of high-frequency words, light text, predictable sentence patterns, and strong visual support.

Level 2 offers early readers a bit more challenge through varied sentences, increased text load, and text-supportive special features.

Level 3 advances early-fluent readers toward fluency through increased text load, less reliance on photos, advancing concepts, longer sentences, and more complex special features.

★ **Blastoff! Universe**

Reading Level

Grade **K**

Grades **1–3**

Grade **4**

This edition first published in 2023 by Bellwether Media, Inc.

No part of this publication may be reproduced in whole or in part without written permission of the publisher. For information regarding permission, write to Bellwether Media, Inc., Attention: Permissions Department, 6012 Blue Circle Drive, Minnetonka, MN 55343.

Library of Congress Cataloging-in-Publication Data

Names: Koestler-Grack, Rachel A., 1973- author.
Title: Rhinoceroses / by Rachel Grack.
Description: Minneapolis, MN : Bellwether Media, Inc., 2023. | Series: Blastoff! Readers. Animals at risk | Includes bibliographical references and index. | Audience: Ages 5-8 | Audience: Grades 2-3 | Summary: "Relevant images match informative text in this introduction to rhinoceroses. Intended for students in kindergarten through third grade"-- Provided by publisher.
Identifiers: LCCN 2022037565 (print) | LCCN 2022037566 (ebook) | ISBN 9798886871197 (library binding) | ISBN 9798886872453 (ebook)
Subjects: LCSH: Rhinoceroses--Conservation--Juvenile literature.
Classification: LCC QL737.U63 K64 2023 (print) | LCC QL737.U63 (ebook) | DDC 599.66/8--dc23/eng/20220809
LC record available at https://lccn.loc.gov/2022037565
LC ebook record available at https://lccn.loc.gov/2022037566

Editor: Kieran Downs   Designer: Brittany McIntosh

Printed in the United States of America, North Mankato, MN.

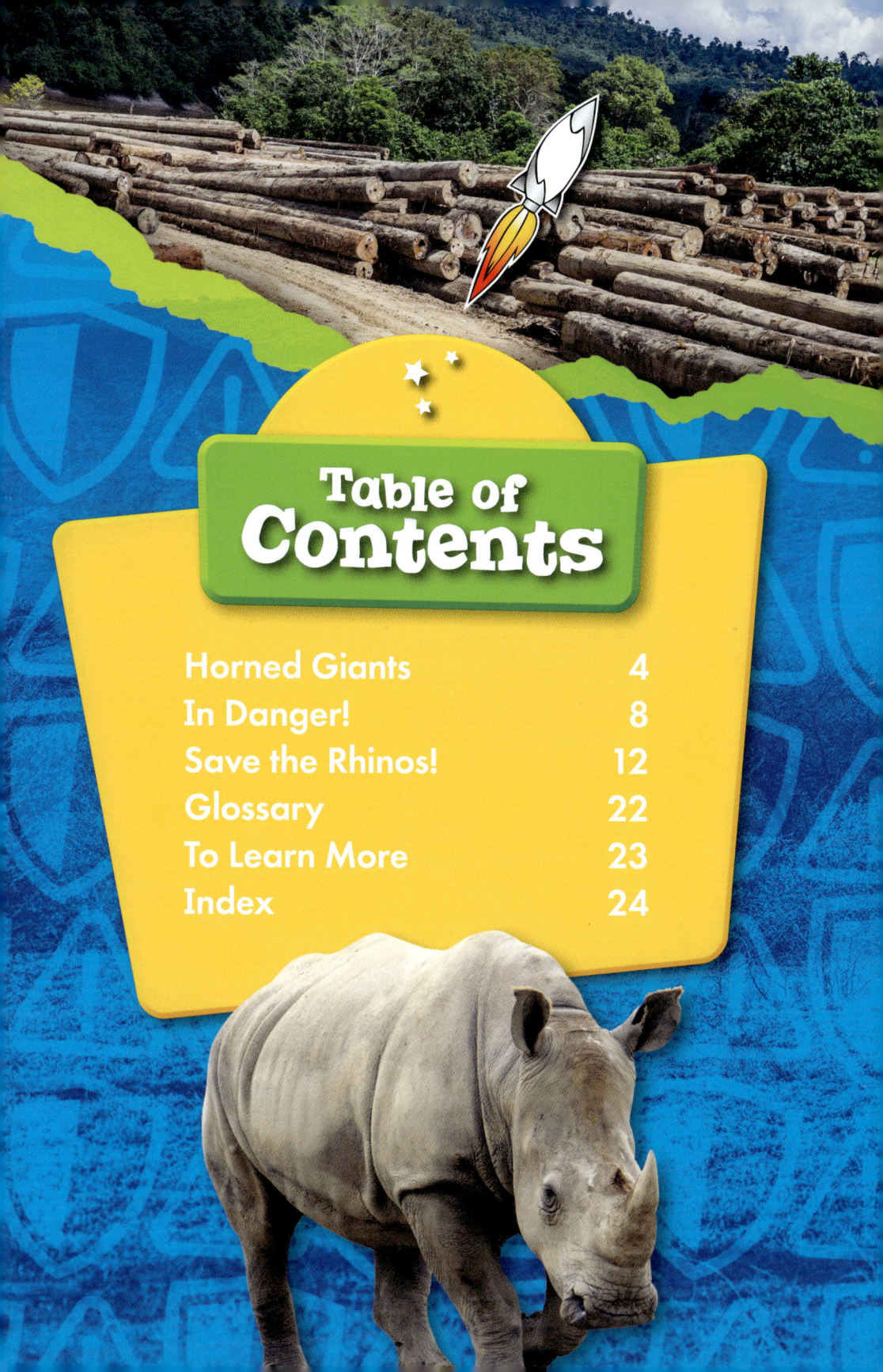

Table of **Contents**

Horned Giants

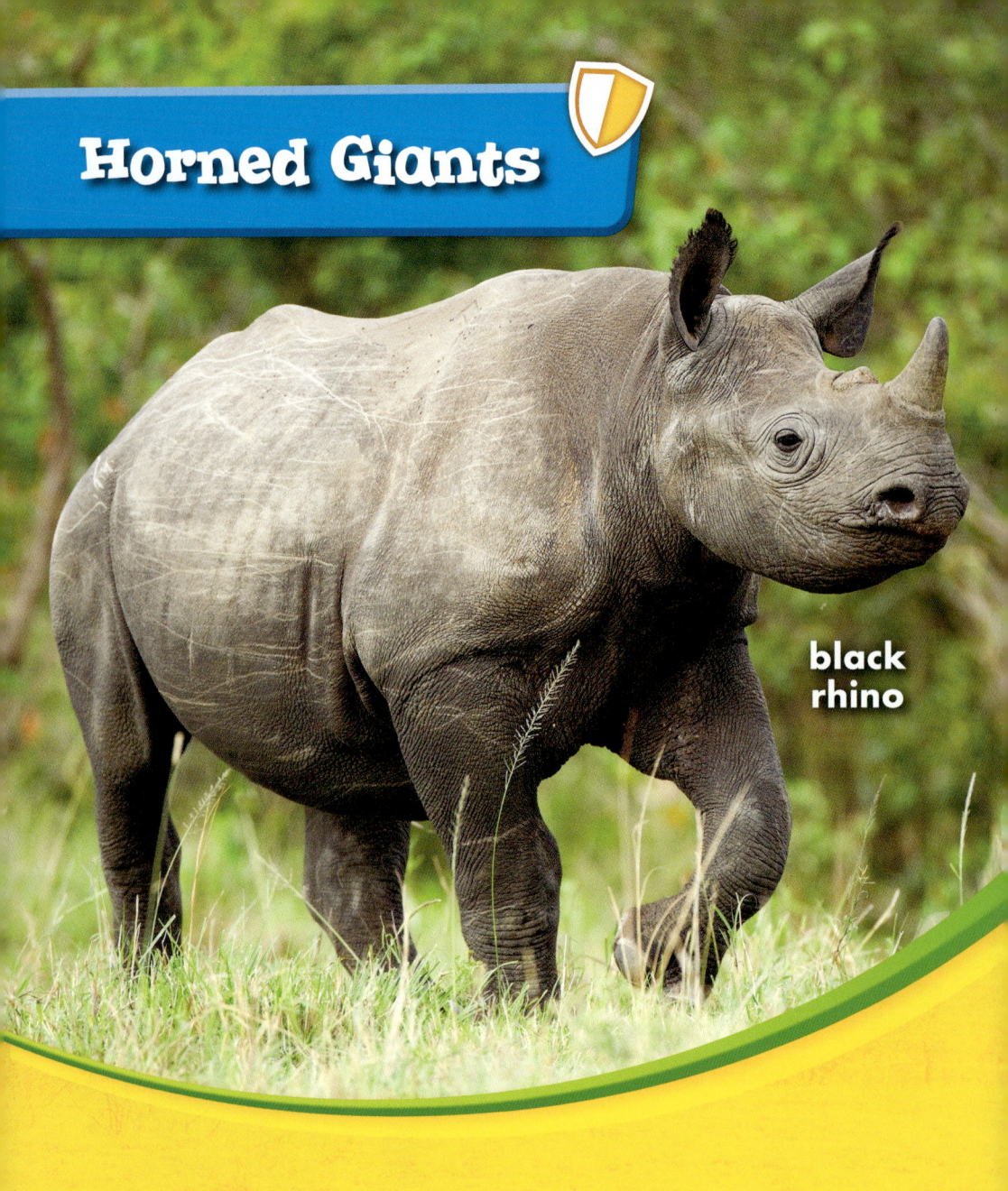

black
rhino

Rhinoceroses are giant, horned animals. They have short, thick legs. They are often called rhinos.

There are five **species** of rhinos. They live in Africa and Asia.

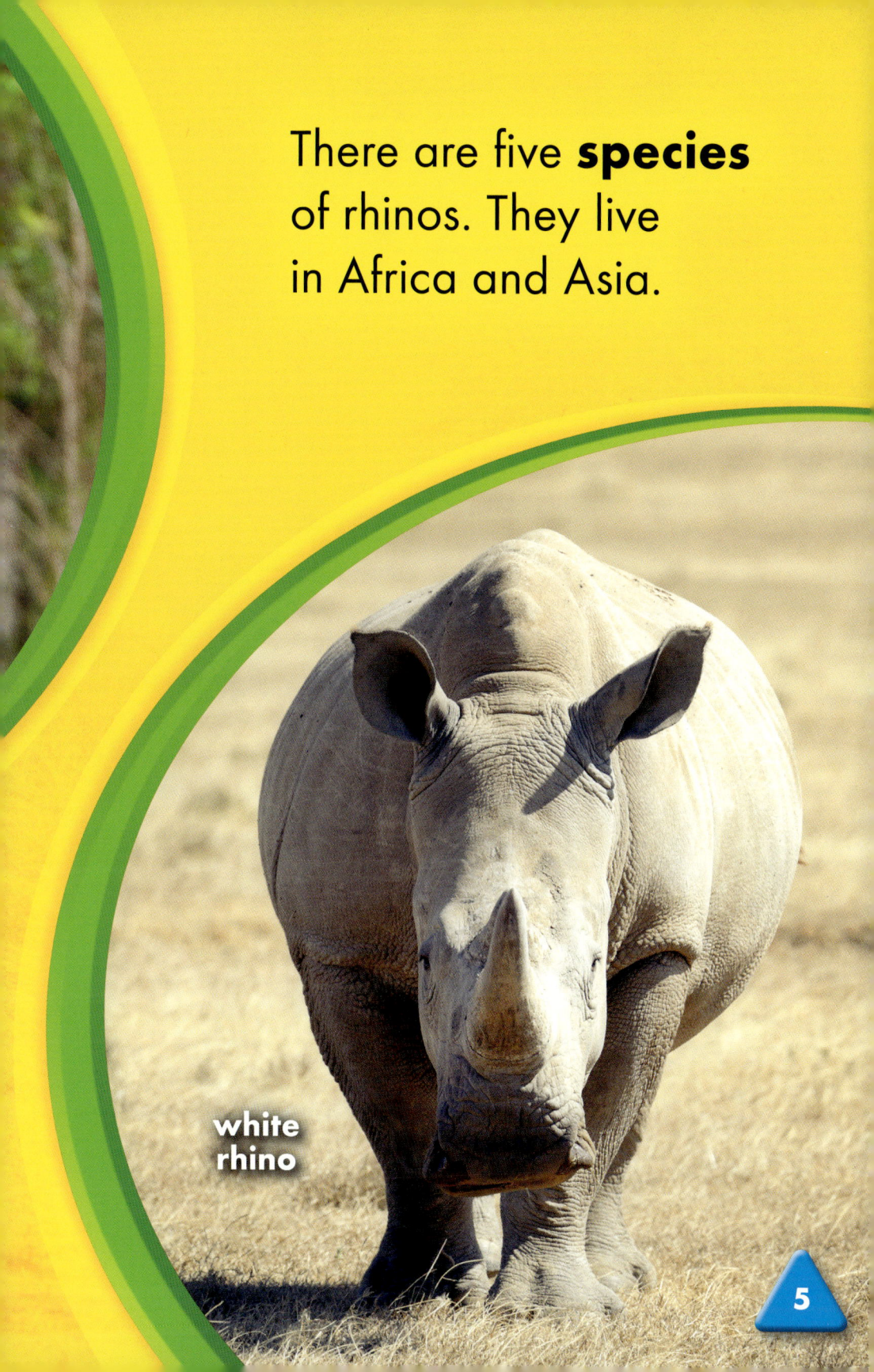

white rhino

5

Forests and grasslands were once full of rhinos. Today, the number of rhinos is smaller. Three species are **critically endangered**.

People have caused
most of their troubles.

Black Rhinoceros Range

range = ◼

N
W · E
S

farmland

Rhinos once had large **home ranges**. But people cleared the land. They built farms and villages. Rhinos lost their homes.

Climate change is also destroying rhino **habitats**.

Threats

1

people need farmland

2

people clear land

3

rhinos lose home ranges

Some people use rhino horns to make **traditional** medicines.

Poachers hunt rhinos for their horns. They sell the horns at high prices.

horn

Black Rhinoceros Stats

Least Concern	Near Threatened	Vulnerable	Endangered	Critically Endangered	Extinct in the Wild	Extinct

conservation status: critically endangered

life span: up to 50 years

11

Save the Rhinos!

greater one-horned rhinos

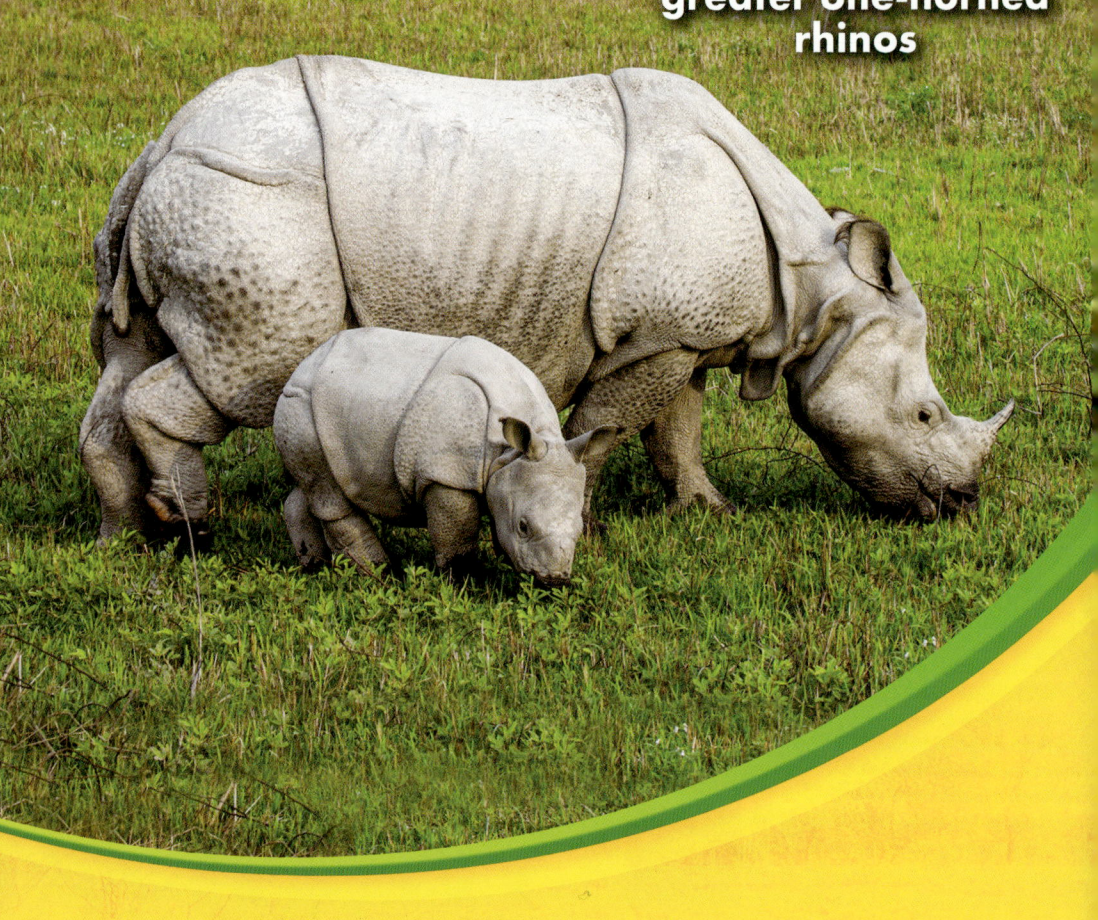

Rhinos eat large amounts of plants. This keeps their **ecosystems** healthy.

Without them, plant life would overgrow. Other animals would suffer, too.

The World with Rhinoceroses

1 more rhinos

2 healthy number of plants

3 healthy land

Many governments pass **laws** to keep rhinos safe. They make it illegal to sell horns.

People are not allowed
to use horns in medicines.

15

Governments set aside land for rhinos. Rhinos are moved to these lands for safety.

moving a rhino

16

Police guard them to stop poachers.

Wildlife groups work to give rhinos larger homes. They make pathways between **reserves**. Rhinos have more room to move.

Sumatran rhino

Their numbers are slowly growing.

Adopting a rhino helps these giant animals in big ways. Using products that do not harm rhino habitats also makes a difference.

Together, everyone can help save rhinos!

Javan rhino

Glossary

adopting—taking over the care for someone or something; people who adopt wild animals give money for someone else to care for them.

climate change—a human-caused change in Earth's weather due to warming temperatures

critically endangered—greatly in danger of dying out

ecosystems—communities of plants and animals living in certain places

habitats—places and natural surroundings in which plants or animals live

home ranges—the lands on which a group of animals lives and travels

laws—rules that must be followed

poachers—people who hunt illegally

reserves—areas of land set aside for wild animals

species—kinds of animals

traditional—related to customs, ideas, or beliefs passed down from one generation to the next

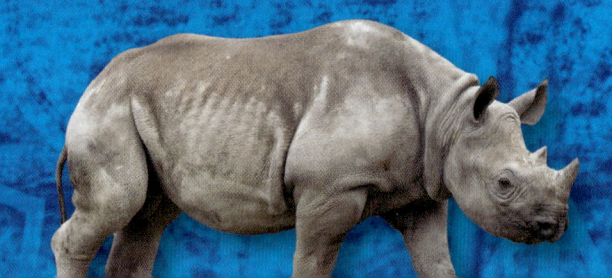

To Learn More

AT THE LIBRARY

Bodden, Valerie. *Rhinoceroses*. Mankato, Minn.: The Creative Company, 2023.

Duling, Kaitlyn. *Rhinoceroses*. Minneapolis, Minn.: Bellwether Media, 2021.

Gillespie, Katie. *Rhino*. New York, N.Y.: AV2, 2022.

ON THE WEB

FACTSURFER

Factsurfer.com gives you a safe, fun way to find more information.

1. Go to www.factsurfer.com.

2. Enter "rhinoceroses" into the search box and click 🔍.

3. Select your book cover to see a list of related content.

Index